? **Essential Question**
What can learning about different cultures teach us?

All the Way from Europe

by Hugh Brown
illustrated by Nick Hardcastle

CHAPTER 1
No More Old Buildings!

Sarah turned off the TV and sighed. Her mother looked up from her laptop. "Had enough?" she asked.

Sarah nodded. "It's as if they're speaking a foreign language," she said.

Her mom laughed, "That's because they are. They're speaking French."

"Yeah, I know," Sarah smiled. Back in North Carolina, Sarah had been excited when her mother told her they were going to Europe. Her mom had some research to do for her work. She said they could do some sightseeing on the side when she was done with work each day.

However, after these first two days in Paris, Sarah wasn't feeling so enthusiastic any more. Why did adults find old buildings so fascinating?

Sarah thought that if she had brought her saxophone, she could have played that, but her mom had said it would be far too loud to practice in hotel rooms.

That afternoon, as they drove to Brussels in Belgium, Sarah tried to read a guidebook about Europe. Most of it was about old buildings again. Sarah closed the book and put it on the back seat. She sighed once more.

"Have you had enough fun for one day?" her mother asked.

"Something like that," Sarah replied, looking very glum.

Sarah's mom thought for a moment, then she suggested, "How about this? When we arrive in a new city, you can have a turn on my laptop. You can do your own research on the places we visit. Then, after I'm done working in the mornings, we'll do what you want in the afternoons. Is it a deal?"

Sarah considered the offer. "I must congratulate you on a wicked idea," she said.

"Complimenting me, are you?" her mom laughed. "You know that compliments give me a big head."

Sarah grinned. "Anyway," she said, "who would name a city after Brussels sprouts?"

Her mother shrugged. "I guess that's something you can find out in your research."

STOP AND CHECK

Why does Sarah's mother suggest a new plan for the vacation?

CHAPTER 2

Saxophones and Hotdogs

The next day, right before lunch, Sarah's mom put down her work and said happily, "Finished! So, what are we doing this afternoon?"

"I think Brussels is going to be cool," Sarah said. "Two of my favorite things come from here. First, you've got Brussels sprouts."

Her mother raised an eyebrow. "That's not what you said the last time I cooked them."

"Got you!" Sarah blurted out. "But I discovered that the city isn't named after them. It's the other way around. Brussels sprouts are named after the city, because this is where they were first grown."

"So what are your two favorite things from here?" asked her mom.

"Tintin is from here! The Tintin stories were written by a Belgian author, and there's even a whole museum here about comics," Sarah replied. "That's my kind of cultural museum."

"And what's the second thing?" her mom asked.

Sarah replied, "You know I love the saxophone. Well, it was invented by a man named Adolphe Sax, who was born near Brussels. The Museum of Musical Instruments has a huge collection of Sax's instruments. And it's supposed to be really fun, with lots of hands-on stuff to do."

Her mother looked a bit disappointed. "That all sounds good," she hesitated, "but ..."

"But what?" Sarah asked playfully. "Oh, I get it. You think I forgot about Belgian chocolate. The third stop on our list is the Museum of Cocoa and Chocolate. For you!"

Her mom brightened up. "Perfect! Let's go."

The next city Sarah and her mom visited was Frankfurt in Germany. "So what's on our agenda this afternoon?" her mom asked.

"There are two things we need to do first," Sarah answered. "There's a communication museum that looks really interesting for kids, and of course we have to buy some hotdogs."

Her mom looked puzzled. "Shouldn't we try some German food while we're here?"

"Frankfurt is the birthplace of ..." Sarah did a little drum roll on the table, "the frankfurter! German immigrants brought them to New York and started selling them in buns. That's when people began calling them hotdogs."

"Well, what are we waiting for? Let's eat some frankfurters!" Sarah's mom exclaimed.

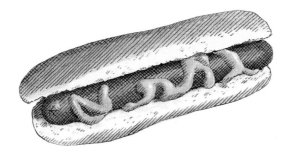

STOP AND CHECK

What did Sarah discover in Brussels and in Frankfurt?

CHAPTER 3
Don't Eat the Hamburgers!

On their way to the next city in Germany, called Hamburg, Sarah noticed a road sign that said "Bremen."

"Why does Bremen sound familiar?" she asked her mom.

"It's that folktale, *The Musicians of Bremen*. I used to read it to you," her mom answered. "It's about those animals that scare the robbers away."

"Oh, I loved that story," Sarah said, smiling as she remembered.

Sarah looked out the window at another town they were passing. "Remember when we were at home looking at the map before we left, and you said we were going to drive to all these different places? I thought they would take us days to reach, but all the countries here are really small compared to the United States."

"It makes you realize just how huge the United States is," her mother said. "In a way, the U.S. is a bit like Europe, and the different states are like the different countries that make up Europe."

"When you think of it like that," Sarah said, "it's no wonder the states are all so different from each other."

Her mother smiled. "I think you've learned something about home while you've been learning about these places in Europe," she commented. Sarah nodded in agreement.

"So," her mother added, "what are we going to see in Hamburg?"

"Well, guess what Hamburg is known for?" Sarah asked her mom.

"Ham?" her mom suggested.

"Very funny," Sarah replied. "It has a great zoo, so today I thought we could visit the animals first, and then look at the Hamburgers in town."

"And once we've looked at the hamburgers, we can eat them," her mom said.

"No!" Sarah contradicted. "We can't eat them!"

"Why not?" her mom asked.

"Because Hamburgers are what the people who live in Hamburg are called," Sarah explained. "The hamburgers we do eat were probably named after the meat patties German immigrants ate in the United States."

"I see," her mother said, looking relieved. "Well, maybe we could look at Hamburgers while eating American-style hamburgers."

"Now you've got it!" Sarah laughed.

STOP AND CHECK

Why does Sarah's mother say the United States is similar to Europe?

CHAPTER 4

Pizza and Soccer

After two days in Hamburg, Sarah and her mom flew to Naples in Italy. As soon as they were settled into their hotel, Sarah took out the laptop.

"What are you doing?" her mom asked.

"Finding out about Naples," Sarah replied.

Sarah's mom smiled. "I think you're enjoying this research. Maybe it's given you a new appreciation of home, too."

"I guess it has," answered Sarah. "In fact, I think when we get home, I'm going to do research on North Carolina. There's probably tons of stuff about it that I don't know."

In the morning while her mom worked, Sarah looked out the window, watching people on the street below.

Finally, her mom finished and said, "Sorry to take so long, honey. I'm done now, and I'm all yours. What's the plan for today?"

Sarah turned from her spot by the window and answered immediately, "Neapolitan pizza! Neapolitan means 'from Naples,' and Naples is famous for its pizza."

Her mother laughed, "And it just happens to be your favorite food, too."

Sarah grinned. "That's just a lucky coincidence."

Sarah and her mom walked to a pizzeria a couple of blocks away from the hotel. After they ordered, they sat at a table outside. In the park across the road, a group of kids about Sarah's age were playing soccer. She wished she could join their game.

Sarah's thoughts were interrupted by the waiter bringing their pizzas. After he left, Sarah's mom whispered, "I think there's been a misunderstanding. This doesn't look like our pizza at home."

Sarah giggled. "I think this is what it's supposed to be like. Doesn't it smell delicious?"

"Well, I don't mean to be critical, but I think they ran out of dough," her mom commented. "The crust is so thin you can barely find it under the tomato sauce and cheese!"

When they had finished eating, Sarah and her mom crossed the road to take a walk in the park. One of the boys playing soccer missed a pass, and the ball rolled toward Sarah. She dribbled the ball and then passed it back to the boy. He called out, *"Grazie!"* which Sarah knew meant "thank you" in Italian. Then he smiled and called out something else in Italian.

"Sorry, I only speak English," she called back. The boy came over.

"Do you come from England?" he asked, switching languages.

"I'm American," Sarah said.

"I was asking if you wanted to play with us," he said.

"Thanks, I'd love to play," she answered, "if it's okay with my mom." She looked at her mom, who nodded yes.

"Good," he said. "But I thought Americans only play football and baseball—oh, and basketball. How do you know how to play soccer?"

"It's like the saxophone, hotdogs, and pizza," Sarah explained as they jogged over to join the others. "They were all brought to America, and later they became some of our favorite things."

STOP AND CHECK

What important things does Sarah learn in Naples?

Summarize

Use the most important details from *All the Way from Europe* to summarize the story. Information from your graphic organizer may help you.

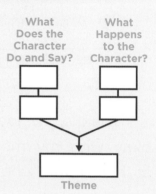

Text Evidence

1. What features of *All the Way from Europe* help you identify it as realistic fiction? GENRE

2. What do Sarah and her mom learn about their own country as they travel? How does this help show the author's main message? THEME

3. What is the meaning of the word *glum* on page 3? Use the cause-and-effect relationships on pages 2–3 to help you figure out the meaning.
CONTEXT CLUES: CAUSE AND EFFECT

4. How did Sarah's attitude change after Chapter 1? Write about how this helps show what the author is trying to tell readers.
WRITE ABOUT READING

Compare Texts
Read about where some sports started.

A SPORTING GIFT

Many sports that we think are as "American as apple pie" actually came from other places.

AMERICAN FOOTBALL

Some say modern American football had its start in 1823 in England. A schoolboy named William Ellis was playing soccer when he picked up the ball and ran with it. That was the beginning of a game called rugby, in which players can carry and throw the ball. Over time, the rugby ball became oval-shaped because that made it easier to carry and pass than a round ball.

In the 1870s, American football was played more like soccer than like rugby. Then schools and universities began to allow players to carry and throw the ball. By the 1880s, these rugby-type rules were popular, and the game that we know as American football was born.

17

BASEBALL

Baseball started out as an English children's game called "rounders." Rounders is played with a round bat, four bases, a bowler (pitcher), and a backstop. English immigrants brought this game to the United States, where it slowly changed.

An American, Abner Doubleday, is often credited with "inventing" baseball in Cooperstown, New York, in 1839. Research shows, however, it is more likely that the modern game's rules were first written down in the 1840s in New York. Alexander Cartwright and three other members of the New York Knickerbockers "base ball" team wrote down all of the "New York rules" of the game. These eventually became the standard rules of baseball played today.

FROM THE UNITED STATES TO THE WORLD

Basketball was invented in 1891 by an American named James Naismith. He wanted to create an indoor game that would be fun to play and keep his students fit during the winter when it was cold outside. Naismith made only 13 rules for how to play basketball, many of which are still part of the game today.

The game was called "basket ball" because the original court used peach-packing baskets for hoops. Unfortunately, the players did not take the bottoms out of the baskets. This meant that every time a goal was scored, someone had to climb up a ladder and retrieve the ball! Basketball, without the peach baskets, is now played all around the world.

Make Connections

What does soccer have in common with American football? ESSENTIAL QUESTION

How do *All the Way from Europe* and *A Sporting Gift* show the way that things and ideas travel from one part of the world to another? TEXT TO TEXT

Focus on Literary Elements

Dialogue Authors use dialogue to show readers what characters say. Dialogue can help move the plot along and show action. Comic strips are an example of the way a story can be told just by using dialogue and illustrations.

Read and Find In this piece of dialogue on page 10, the author tells us what the characters say and what they are doing. As you read it, think about the images that could help tell the story.

"And once we've looked at the hamburgers, we can eat them," her mom said.

"No!" Sarah contradicted. "We can't eat them!"

"Why not?" her mom asked.

"Because Hamburgers are what the people who live in Hamburg are called," Sarah explained.

Your Turn

Now turn this or another four lines of dialogue into a comic strip. Use the words the characters say and add your own drawings. You can work with a partner or on your own. Share your comic strip with your classmates.